Not My Shame
A True Story

by

SHEILA RAE BOYD

© 2020 Sheila Rae Boyd, All Rights Reserved.

Editing, Layout, and Cover Design by Sheila R. Boyd, EdD, sheilaraeboyd@gmail.com.

No part of this publication may be reproduced, stored in a retrieval system, or transmitted in any form by any means electronic, mechanical, photocopying, recording, or otherwise, except brief extracts for the purpose of review, without written permission from the copyright owner.

A Note from the Author

This is a completely true story. However, I have changed the names of all the people in this story in respect to their privacy except for the name of my first husband . . .

I used his real name.

Table of Contents

A Note from the Author 3
Introduction 7
Chapter 1 11
Chapter 2 17
Chapter 3 21
Chapter 4 25
Chapter 5 31
Chapter 6 37
Chapter 7 41
Chapter 8 47
Chapter 9 51
Chapter 10 55
Chapter 11 59
Chapter 12 63
Chapter 13 69
Chapter 14 75
Afterword 77

 Introduction

"Blessed be God, even the Father of our Lord Jesus Christ, the Father of mercies, and the God of all comfort; Who comforteth us in all our tribulation, that we may be able to comfort them which are in any trouble, by the comfort wherewith we ourselves are comforted of God." *(2 Corinthians 2:3, 4)*

God has given each of us "a story." It is a highly personal treasure, a journey, a life of experiences that matches no other. In our minds, we can spread out those experiences like cards on a table in order to inspect them as individual events, sorting out some we want to remember and wishing we could forget others. Some of them bring us great joy; others embrace some of our greatest sorrows. But it is the sum of these events that makes us each who we are.

I can speak the language of losing a child, of having multiple miscarriages, of having a husband turn his back on our family and walk away with another man, because those events are a part of my story. But I cannot speak the language, for example, of suffering through cancer: it is not an event that God, up to this time in my life, has chosen for me to experience. You see, each of our stories is unique to us, in order for us to be a comfort to those with whom we have and will come in contact.

Recently, someone who knows me quite well and familiar with my story made the comment, "Well, THAT story needs to be put in a box, buried, and never brought up again!" He was referring to the story of my first marriage.

However, does God want us to bury our story? Should we turn our faces away from it in shame?

I told the person who made that comment, "I will not bury it; it is not my shame. I will use it to help others experiencing a similar story." For some reason it was as though he wanted me to feel ashamed of what I've been through. I didn't choose this story; God, in His infinite wisdom, chose it for me.

I believe God actually wants us to shout from the rooftop our story, with all its wonder and its ugliness, for in revealing our story to others, (1) we give a loving Heavenly Father the glory for seeing us through those experiences, and (2) we are able to bring comfort, wisdom, and support to others going through a similar experience, thereby giving them hope!

Because I've refused to bury my story but instead have owned it, I've had the beautiful opportunity to speak to several ladies who are going through miscarriage, or the loss of a child, or the loss of a husband to homosexuality. It brings joy to my heart that God can take such ugliness and allow me to "be able to comfort them . . . by the comfort wherewith we ourselves are comforted of God."

Don't bury your story! No matter how dreadful it may seem to you, it will be a beautiful treasure for those who need to hear it!

This is a part of my story . . .

# Chapter 1

I stopped breathing. My heart pounded. I stared at my husband of more than 10 years and the father of my three children sitting across the table from me. I'm not sure how long I sat like that, trying to process the information he had just given me.

Suddenly, I thought I was going to vomit. I focused on my renewed breathing to keep from losing everything in my stomach. Something inside of me told me to cry, but no tears would come—I was too shocked. All I could comprehend was that I couldn't get enough air into my lungs.

But let's back up . . .

He was my childhood sweetheart, and we married when we were both 19 years old after two years into college. We met in a very large Baptist church in Indianapolis, Indiana. My family had attended the church from the time I started fifth grade. We were there every time the church doors were open. Sometimes, it seemed it was our real home.

I first saw Walter Parks when a gentleman in the church who typically picked him up on Sundays to bring him to church was unable to do so one particular Sunday and approached my father about filling in for him. My dad accepted, and our family picked up Walter the first time the following Sunday. Over the next several months, we gave him transportation to church several times on Sunday mornings.

Our youth department boasted an attendance of approximately 200 teenagers by the time we entered high school. Being the same age, Walter and I saw a lot of each other at church-sponsored youth events that the church arranged, even though I did have a couple of dates with other guys during that time.

Walter exuded a very charismatic personality. It seemed that everyone, including our youth pastor and our pastor, loved him. The girls all but swooned over him. He was certainly the subject of many of their conversations when he was not within earshot. He was as active as he could be in the youth department given that he had no transportation to church of his own. He many times rode the city bus to and from church and church activities.

I, on the other hand, was a very quiet, shy girl; and although I thought he was quite dashing, I believed I never had a shot in capturing his attention. In fact, one time after Walter and I had been dating for a while, I entered the girls' restroom at the church just in time to overhear some teen girl say to the others, "How did Sheila get Walter? I mean, he's so outgoing, I would never guess they would be dating each other!"

My brother and Walter eventually became quite close friends, hanging around together at various church activities. At one point, Walter asked my brother about my outgoing, younger sister and indicated he would like to date her; however, she was dating someone else at the time. So, my brother suggested he could introduce him to his "other sister." Walter was unaware Johnny had another sister, but he agreed to the introduction. Although he didn't actually ask me for a date, we did "hang out" at youth events from time to time or sat close enough to talk on the bus ride to some church activity, sometimes while he sat with a girl he actually did ask out on a date. It seemed we enjoyed each other's company, and it was easy to talk about most any subject.

Each summer our youth department took a large number of teens to youth camp. When we were 16 years old, we both, along with my brother, attended the youth camp. Walter entered a preaching contest for teen boys, in which he won first place. I sat in the audience and listened to him; I was quite impressed at how well he preached and was able to easily get spiritual principles across to the teens listening. As the contest drew to a close, I approached him to compliment him on his preaching when a group of giggly, young girls descended upon him, gushing their praise. Too shy to try to navigate through the sea of female bodies, I hung back and eventually just turned and left.

Much to my surprise, my brother hunted me down in the campground that afternoon and told me Walter wanted to see me about something. He knowingly grinned, but wouldn't tell me the reason for Walter wanting to meet with me. I went to the designated place. Walter seemed nervous, but finally was able to get out that he would like to take me bowling at the bowling alley on the campground after the evening service. I was shocked, but extremely happy to accept his invitation . . . although I had never been bowling in my life.

I was so nervous at being on an actual date with Walter that the first ball I attempted to roll down the alley toward the triangle of pins at the other end, flew off my hand backwards and almost hit him in the head! I wanted to die!

We started seeing more of each other, always at church functions. Since he had no transportation, he still usually rode the city bus to church and church-sponsored events; I got in the habit of waiting for him in the church lobby, and we would then sit together. A few times church or a church activity would run too late for him to catch the bus to ride home, so my dad would drive him home. Both my parents grew to really like him. His tenacity to be at church greatly impressed them.

Walter and I each graduated from our individual high schools within a few days of each other, he attending my graduation and my family and I attending his. College loomed in the near future. We chose to attend the same college, Baptist Bible College in Springfield, Missouri. Walter's desire was to become a pastor. He had shared with me that at one time before he accepted the Lord as his Savior that he had wanted to become a

Catholic priest. He was never a Catholic, but he seemed to love people and wanted to serve others. Now that he had accepted the Lord, becoming a pastor fit into what his motivation and passion dictated.

Chapter 2

We were finally off to college! Since neither of us had a vehicle and Missouri was a long way from home (we figured about an eight-hour drive), Walter's grandparents offered to drive us out there, along with a small trailer filled with our luggage and boxes. This was the longest we had been in each other's company at one time, but we really had a lot of fun. His grandparents were fun people to be around, as well; and the trip seemed more like a vacation.

The rules at college seemed harsh. I thought my parents were strict! Girls were not supposed to even speak to guys except during designated date times, which, for the most part, were Friday evenings and Sunday afternoons/evenings. Walter and I ended up seeing less of each other than we did when we lived at home. We did attend the same church, so we were able to sit together during church services and ride the church bus together to and from church. The college had a rule that even on dates there must be an extra girl (chaperone). Luckily, I had a roommate who rarely dated, but was eager to get out of our room for a couple of hours here and there to accompany Walter and I on dates. Even after we left college, she remained one of my best friends.

Walter quickly became well-known at college. He was very active in extracurricular activities, including martial arts, a pseudo-fraternity that met on campus, some kind of preaching club, and other activities. Sometimes the other activities "bit" into our dating opportunities, but we still made the time to see each other as often as we could.

The thing I remember the most during that time when it came to our relationship was that we always had so much fun! We talked together, laughed together, enjoyed music together. We prayed together, read God's Word together, and just enjoyed sharing our dreams, our fears, our childhood memories with one another and became very close: we were best friends.

He was always super attentive to me and protective of me (he always made a big deal of walking on the side of the sidewalk that was next to the street in Springfield—that way a vehicle would hit him first if one strayed off the road). He constantly wrote me little love notes and hid them where I would find them later. He bought or simply made little gifts for me regularly.

Coming from a very tumultuous home that eventually led to my parents divorcing, I could not believe how wonderful Walter's and my relationship was. It was everything warm and beautiful. It was settling; it was peaceful; it was loving.

The college prohibited freshmen becoming engaged at school. They were to wait until their first year ended so as not to distract them from their studies. However, Walter and I talked of marriage a lot. We had dated more than two years by this time. We both wanted children very much. We even brought up the subject that if something happened that we were not able to have children, would adoption be a viable option? We both answered with a resounding "Yes!" We planned that a second year of college under our belts before marriage would make a wise decision. We dreamed of Walter eventually pastoring a church and I serving in whatever capacities I could as his wife at his side. Actually, we made a great team in everything we endeavored.

Just a few days before our first year of college ended, our church took a bus load of college students to Silver Dollar City in Branson, Missouri, for the day. On our way to Silver Dollar City, Walter pulled out an engagement ring and asked me on the bus to marry him. The whole bus went up in cheers. My face turned every shade of red there is, but I said, "Yes!" He put the ring on my finger and quickly brushed a kiss over my lips—kissing was prohibited by the school! I can't remember much more about that day; I just kept looking at the most beautiful ring I had ever seen sitting on my left hand.

Before starting college, I had worked jobs at home to save up to pay for my first year completely. I had turned down a full scholarship to a business school in Indianapolis because I wanted to go to a Bible college. My parents could not afford to send me to college, so if I went, I knew it was up to me financially to find a way.

When I arrived in Springfield, I had most of my first year already paid in advance, with enough reserve to pay for the rest later on. I only had to find ways to pay for incidentals along the way.

However, second year was another story . . . plus, I had a wedding to start planning for the end of that year! I was thrilled to find a job on campus, working as a "floor mom" that would pay for all my second year. Working on campus solved another problem: I still did not have a vehicle, so at least I didn't have to drive to work! However, having a job had a downside to it: less time to see Walter. He also procured a job on campus, working in the cafeteria; but working, extracurricular activities, class, and studying took up just about all his time. About the only time we saw each other was in church.

Chapter 3

There were two other guys on campus who tried to get me to go on a date with them, but I was proud to hold up my left hand and say, "I'm engaged!"

One of the guys was an on-campus maintenance man. He was given the job to change out all the door handles of the rooms on the floor for which I was the "floor mom." Since it was a girls' dorm and guys were not allowed, I was to stay with him the whole time he was on the floor working. We ended up spending quite a few hours together as he worked and I watched . . . but we ended up getting into quite a deep conversation about relationships in general and what kind of relationship we each wanted in the future. He finally seemed to get to what seemed his goal from the start: he asked me to go on a date with him.

Before I could answer him, he broke out into singing "Cherish," looking up at me every few seconds. He had a great voice! He ended with, "So how about you going out with me this Friday night?"

I held up my left hand and said, "I'm engaged!"

He responded that he knew that I was engaged and to whom I was engaged. He warned me that maybe I should re-think my engagement to Walter . . . that he had heard things. He didn't elaborate; and I dismissed his caution, thinking he was just being competitive, trying to get a date with me.

You must understand that I grew up in a very strict Christian environment. I was strongly protected by my parents, especially my mother, from many things to which today's children of even very young ages are not only exposed, but are fluent in their understanding of them. She was extremely controlling and strict over every area of my and my siblings' lives. We were not allowed to date apart from church events and then only after the age of 16; we were not allowed to swim with anyone of the opposite sex; we were not allowed to wear shorts; we were not allowed to ever go off in a vehicle with any other teen, boy or girl; we were not allowed to go to school functions, especially dances; we were never allowed to talk on the phone, etc. For example, I would have been able to quote a dictionary definition of the word "homosexuality" but as I had had no personal exposure to it in any form, I can say now I certainly had no understanding of it.

I'm not saying this was a bad thing; it is simply a fact that it was the type of upbringing under which I grew up. I was to later learn that I was the perfect type of person that many sexual predators or people with certain sexual addictions or secret, parallel lifestyles look for to partner up with, especially if they desire to have children of their own. That thought shocked me when I was first confronted with it: that this type of people actually look for someone with my specific type of upbringing with which to partner for the purpose of having children!

During our second year of college, Walter was ecstatic that he got a job as the elevator operator at the historic downtown hotel, working evenings and nights. He regularly shared rich stories of some of the patrons, a few of whom were celebrities. One day I was stunned when he shared with me that a male patron of the hotel had solicited him for sex on more than one occasion. Actually, he shared that story with me several different times over a period of time. It seemed to me he almost bragged that someone would approach him like that. It was my first exposure of any kind regarding homosexuality; and just the thought of it sickened me, but I never even imagined that Walter would ever even think of taking someone up on an offer of that kind. After all, he would become a preacher soon!

Later that same year Walter shared with me another story that often puzzled me as to why he felt the need to share it with me. Again, this was a story he repeated to me on more than one occasion. He remarked that in the boys' dorm one evening a meeting of some kind had been called, so several of the guys assembled together. It was almost bedtime, so most of the guys were dressed for bed. While they were standing, listening to whomever called the meeting, Walter said a guy that we both knew (he had grown up in the same church in Indianapolis as we had) was wearing boxer shorts at the meeting and that his privates had fallen out of them. I remember thinking, "Why are you telling me this? Why is this something I need to know?" I chalked it up to "male humor" of some kind.

One day, Walter and I and my roommate were walking together down a sidewalk of Springfield, Missouri. We were having a great time as we walked, talking and laughing and just having fun. I noticed a man in the far distance walking toward us on the same sidewalk. As we continued walking, of course the man got closer. Finally, he passed us and went on his way, as we did ours.

Suddenly Walter spoke, "That man that just passed us . . ."

I said, "Yeah."

He responded, "He is a homosexual."

I turned and looked at the guy. He looked like any guy walking down the street to me. My roommate agreed with me.

Walter explained, "His eyes and mine met as he walked past. The way he looked at me let me know he is homosexual."

I said, "What?!"

He repeated what he had said.

I remember responding that if Walter was not a homosexual (which I just took for granted was the truth), why would that guy try to catch his eye? I mean, he didn't try to "catch my eye" or "catch my roommate's eye." I mean, I understood my roommate and I were both female, but what did Walter mean by "the way the guy looked at him"? It didn't make any sense to me.

Chapter 4

My parents were going through a divorce. My whole childhood I had listened to so many shouting matches between them, as well as witness physical violence. I saw them go to marriage counselors to no avail. I saw them talk to our pastor numerous times, again to no avail.

I knew I wanted a different kind of marriage—one that would endure the test of time. I believed with my whole heart that Walter and I would have that. In my mind, we had such a beautiful relationship that was loving, kind, and wholesome and based on Scriptural principles. It was something I prayed about consistently. I prayed that if Walter was not the one the Lord wanted me to marry that He would allow me to see that without any confusion and give me the courage to end the relationship. Even on our wedding day, I remember praying that very morning that the Lord would somehow allow me to see it if I was not to marry Walter and that He would bring about the circumstances and truth that would stop the wedding before it was too late. When I walked down the aisle later that afternoon, I had every confidence that we were meant to be together and that our marriage would endure.

The second year of college had ended; we raced home to Indianapolis and got married at our home church; and we raced back to college as we both had jobs waiting on us for the summer. We moved into an upstairs apartment in an old house in the urban part of Springfield, Missouri.

We still did not own a vehicle, so married life was a little rough and extremely busy going from classes to work to home. I worked afternoons into the evening. Walter worked nights at a nursing home, barely getting home in time to change clothes and we dash to the campus for class. If I got home from work even five minutes late in the evening, we would miss seeing each other that day. Weekends were filled with carrying laundry to a laundromat and carrying it back home wet to hang out on the line to save money on drying and with grocery shopping, carrying the bags of groceries many blocks back to our apartment.

Finally, graduation came, and Walter was offered a job as the music director/youth pastor/assistant pastor at a small church in Texas. We ended up being there only three months as we caught the pastor stealing from the church. I was not emotionally or physically well at the time, having miscarried our first child and almost dying in the process. We left there and went to a small rural church in northern Illinois that was the home church of my former college roommate. She was now the church secretary. Even though they could not pay him, the church "hired" Walter as music director/youth pastor/assistant pastor.

Life was extremely busy. Walter was a very active youth pastor, having almost weekly youth activities, while preparing Sunday lessons and sometimes preaching in place of the pastor, as well as working a fulltime, night-shift job. Everyone loved him. Other pastors and youth workers from around the state and more were beginning to meet him, and they loved him and highly respected him, as well. I was proud to be his wife.

I was still healing from my miscarriage and spent a lot of time with my former roommate working in the church office or wherever the pastor needed us to work. It worked out well for Walter and I since he slept during the day after working all night. My former roommate and I did the office work, wrote and directed VBS, set up and ran a printing shop in the church basement, held outdoor Bible clubs in various neighborhoods during the summer, and more.

Less than two years later, my sister and her husband moved to a small town in northern Indiana where my brother-in-law became the new pastor of a church. He offered for Walter and I to move there and Walter become the music director/youth pastor/assistant pastor.

Walter had already set up a fairly large network of pastors and youth leaders in Illinois. He was becoming well-known to many churches and their leaders for his outgoing leadership and style of preaching. Young people flocked to him naturally.

It seemed our marriage was strong, and I could not picture my life to be any better than it was. In Indiana, I did experience two more miscarriages, which each almost resulted in my death. Then I had three premature babies, the last of which we lost. Walter even preached at our daughter's funeral. As tragic and hard as it was to go through, it seemed it brought Walter and I even closer in our relationship. We cried together, prayed together, and got through it together. He was my strength through it all. Eventually, we had the wonderful opportunity to adopt a baby girl, making our family a family of five.

My sister, brother-in-law, Walter, and I grew really close. We were together most of the time. Of course, the four of us were constantly at the church working, our kids playing or even sleeping close by; and we lived only a couple of blocks from each other. My sister played the organ; I played the piano. I had gone through my pregnancies there, and my sister had been a real rock for me through all that. We babysat for each other. We regularly ate at each other's homes, and my sister and I did our weekly grocery shopping together. We gardened together in her vast garden and even had yard sales together. She lost a daughter just two weeks prior to our losing our daughter. We even buried them next to each other in the cemetery. The four of us were practically inseparable.

My sister's four boys were especially fond of Walter. When he walked into their house, all four of them were all over him, trying to wrestle with him, box him, pull him to the floor, etc. On many occasions Walter would go to their bedrooms, shut the door, and spend time with them one-on-one. They seemed to idolize him.

Chapter 5

Walter was now becoming very well-known in Indiana. He was sought after to speak at conferences and special meetings. Troubled teens were brought to him for counsel. He would light up a room when he walked in. He always had a circle of teens gathered around him, laughing, talking, touching him, vying for his attention. He was known to grab a teen boy around the neck and wrestle him to the floor in fun or play-box each other. When Walter and teens were around, it was all fun . . . or so I thought.

At one point during the years we were in northern Indiana, his "manhandling" of teen boys did start to bother me some. I brought up the subject to him one night as we drove home from church. I explained I understood teen boys were many times physical with one another in play and that I could see how that could spill over to their actions toward their youth leader who was popular and well-liked, but couldn't it be translated by others to be a bit too much of "hands on" to a parent or other adult observing it? Homosexuality, although seldom talked about when we first started in the ministry, was beginning to become a subject that was broached in news media, as well as in churches. I wondered if an adult would entertain the idea that Walter might be homosexual.

Walter adamantly refuted each point I brought up to the point I felt if I continued trying to press my point, he might become angry, which would be a real rarity for him. I finally felt like I had exhausted what I was trying to get across to him and that the subject was closed with Walter's indicating that he would not change how he interacted with teen boys because he saw no need to do so.

There was a particular teen boy in our youth department who was struggling in his life. He was a very good-looking teen boy with a super outgoing personality, for whom the girls went crazy over. He fought drug addiction and drinking, and his parents were careworn over him. Walter started counseling him and trying to give him more attention. He would pick up "Jerry" from time to time to take him out for a hamburger or go here or go there with him. It got to be if Walter was not home, he was with Jerry. We had at the time two small babies and we had just lost our daughter, so my hands and my mind were quite occupied with our family to have the time to even take a lot of notice about the time Walter and Jerry were spending together at who knew where.

On at least two occasions, someone came to our bedroom window in the middle of the night and softly tapped on it. Walter would simply get up, get dressed, and leave the house. The first time it happened, I questioned him as to who tapped on the window and where did he go. He said Jerry had needed him, so he came and tapped on the window to let Walter know he wanted to "talk." So, Walter would get dressed; and he and Jerry would go off somewhere together to "talk." He expressed his apology for waking me; they were trying to be quiet enough to let me sleep. I wondered why it was Jerry needed to talk in the middle of the night rather than waiting until morning.

Several times, someone from the church came to our home looking for Walter to ask him a question or request his help with something, and I would say he was over at the church. They would say that no, he was not at the church; they had just come from the church and he was not there. It seemed it became more and more often that Walter was "missing." All of this came back to my mind later on.

The time came when my brother-in-law accepted the pastorate at an Illinois church, and the church in Indiana offered the pastorate of that church to Walter. We had been there quite a few years by that time, and he accepted the position.

One spring we attended a conference in Springfield, Missouri. We met a family—a husband, wife, and very young son. "Henry" was getting ready to graduate from Baptist Bible College in a few days. He indicated he did not know where he was going upon graduation, but that he wanted to work fulltime in a church until he felt he was ready to pastor his own church. I was puzzled at how quickly it all happened being that we had just met this family, but Walter offered Henry and his family to move to Indiana and become the youth pastor at our church, the position that Walter had recently vacated. Henry immediately accepted; and within a very short time, they had moved to our little town.

They were at our church quite a few months. Henry's wife, "Liz," and I became good friends. Our two families would have get-togethers to cook out or go to each other's home for a meal and fun. The four of us became quite close.

One day I saw Liz pull up outside our house with their young boy in tow. I met her at the door, and I could see something was clearly wrong. It appeared she had been crying. Henry and Liz had a rather tumultuous marriage at times, so I assumed she and Henry had argued. As I started to close the door behind her as she came in, I noticed it appeared her car was loaded down with boxes and luggage. It puzzled me.

Liz walked into my kitchen and sat down at the table. She told me almost immediately she was on her way out of town; she was leaving Henry.

I said, surprised, "What?"

She nodded her head. "I'm leaving," she repeated.

"Why?" I asked, alarmed.

She searched my face for a moment. I just kept looking at her.

Finally, she said, "I walked in on Henry last night."

Here, she really started crying. I took her hand.

I repeated back to her, "You walked in on Henry last night?" hoping to get her to open up more.

She nodded her head.

"Yes. I came home early, and he was on the couch. He . . . he . . ."

It seemed she couldn't even say whatever was on her mind.

So, I repeated again, "He was on the couch and...?"

Again, she nodded her head. "Yes, he was on the couch with . . . with . . . someone. And our son was there, also."

I was shaken. "You're kidding!" was all I could think to say.

I would never have imagined Henry having an affair with someone.

She looked back at me hard. "No, I'm not kidding. And I can't stay there anymore. I'm not leaving my son there. I've got to go!"

I waited to see if she would say more and tried to figure out what to say back to her.

"Oh, Liz, I'm so sorry!" I felt it was a lame thing to say, but it was all I could come up with.

"It's worse," she added.

I looked back at her.

"He was having sex with . . . a . . . with a man!"

She put her head down on her hands and shook in sobs.

It was several years later that I learned the man her husband was having sex with that night was my husband, Walter. She had come to tell me, but then chickened out of telling me it was with Walter. She came to my house originally wanting to know if I knew. However, she realized when she started talking, that I didn't know; and she did not want to be the one to tell me.

Chapter 6

One Saturday we traveled to Illinois to visit my sister and brother-in-law and their five children, which we did about once a month or so. We would spend the day with them and then drive back home to Indiana that evening.

Walter had been shut up with all four boys in one of their bedrooms most of the morning. Laughing, shouting, trash talking, etc. could be heard coming from the room, which was the norm. After a couple of hours in there, Walter emerged. He asked my sister if he could walk the boys to an ice cream shop several blocks down the street. She agreed to it, so they took off. I looked out the window as they walked down the street.

Suddenly, I realized Walter had his shirt on backwards! His shirt had a bold design on it, and I thought to myself that there was no way we would have left home without my noticing he had that shirt on backwards. It puzzled me.

I yelled out the window, "Walter, you have your shirt on backwards!"

He looked down and sheepishly pulled his shirt off and put it back on correctly. But it just stuck in me as to why or how that could have happened. I asked myself if he had taken off his shirt in the boys' room; and if he did, why?

Another incident that didn't quite seem what I was told it was happened about this time. My sister's oldest son came to stay with us for a short time. I put our three children in one bedroom and gave him the vacated one. One evening Walter went into his room and closed the door. They were in there for some time. I finally became curious and went up the stairs. I heard noise coming from the room that piqued my curiosity. I went to the door and listened. At first I heard nothing. Then I heard the rumble of their voices, but could not make out what either of them was saying. Suddenly, Walter opened the door . . . and there I stood.

He asked gruffly, "What are you doing?"

I was honest. I said, "I was listening. I wondered why you were in there so long, and I thought I heard you talking so I was trying to hear what you were talking so long about."

Walter came up with some reason that "Max" was struggling with things going on in his life at that time and that he was trying to counsel him and help him by talking things out. In my naivety, I simply accepted what he said.

Walter came to me one day and said he had been struggling with something. He said he thought the Lord was calling him to leave the Indiana church and become a missionary to Australia. Things started falling into place quickly. We traveled back to Springfield, Missouri, to be approved to go out as missionaries under their supervision and almost immediately started deputation to raise our support to go to Australia. An elderly widow in our church offered to buy a motorhome for us to borrow while on deputation so our family could travel together. We were so grateful to her. We sold everything we owned except our clothes and the few things we needed to outfit the motorhome for a family of five to live in.

We had been on the road in a motorhome for 14 months. We were waiting on our passports to arrive, and we knew our time in the States was soon coming to an end. We had about a week of time in-between speaking engagements in Indiana churches, so I suggested we go to my sister's home to spend a few days. We would park our motorhome there and live in it, but would have the availability for me to spend time with her and her children before we left for Australia.

Our time there seemed to go way too fast. We were spending every minute we could with our two families doing things together.

One morning my sister came up with a proposal. She said her husband was going to be gone that day until late at night, preaching at another church. They had a family pass to the local YMCA, and there were a lot of things we could do there. She wondered if we would like to walk there after an early supper. She had found someone to babysit the younger children in her home. She suggested Walter take the two older boys and supervise them, allowing them to spend some last time with him; and that would leave her and I to spend time together without the kids. It was set.

My sister and I spent a couple of hours or so at the YMCA and decided we were ready to go home. She knew the guys would probably stay longer, but Walter would see they got home okay.

Chapter 7

I took my children to the motorhome and put them to bed for the night and waited for Walter to get home. It got later and later. I was beginning to get a little worried when he finally showed up. He seemed jovial, and he indicated he and the boys had had a really good time, describing all the things they had done while at the YMCA.

We started getting ready for bed when, suddenly, my sister knocked on the door to our motorhome.

"Where is 'Jason'?" she asked, looking directly at Walter.

"I don't know," Walter answered, shrugging his shoulders.

"Well, he was with you," she responded. "Didn't he walk home with you?"

I noticed Walter was really nervous and somewhat fidgety.

He stammered, "Well, truth is he got mad at me about something, and he stormed out on his own. I thought he came back home. If he didn't come home ahead of us, I don't know where he is."

By this time, it was almost midnight. I could see the deep fear in my sister's face.

"I've got to go find him!" she said.

"I'll go with you," Walter offered.

"No, you stay here. If he got mad at you, then I don't want you coming with me trying to find him."

Much later, my sister came back to our motorhome to let us know she had found Jason getting ready to jump off a bridge to kill himself. She had been able to stop him just in time!

My mind could not wrap itself around what she had just said. My nephew and I were quite close, and I couldn't imagine what could possibly have driven him to attempt such a thing. When I questioned Walter what they had argued about, he only answered it was just a teen thing of no consequence really—it certainly had "nothing to do with his trying to commit suicide."

The next morning, my brother-in-law was home. He and my sister decided to have a family meeting over at the church with the two of them and their son to discuss the events of the night before. They requested Walter be there, as well. I was asked to babysit the remaining children in their home.

I was so glad Walter was going to be in on the meeting, as he had a great track record for helping troubled teens. I was confident they could get my nephew to open up and set him on the road to having a less stressful life.

While I was babysitting, the phone rang. I answered it. Of all things, it was my mother on the other end of the line. I explained to her that my sister, brother-in-law, and Walter, as well as Jason were all over at the church having a meeting. At this point, I didn't want to tell her that Jason had tried to commit suicide the night before.

My mother started acting strange on the phone.

Finally, she said, "I only wish I could be there for you."

I literally held out the receiver and looked at it.

I answered her, "ME? Why me?"

My mind started racing. How did any of this have anything to do with me? All of a sudden, I was filled with fear! What on earth was going on?

My mother started, "So, they haven't told you yet?" She started crying.

"Told me what?" I demanded.

"Oh, I can't tell you . . ." She hung up.

It seemed like hours before I saw Walter coming across the church lawn toward the house and our motorhome. I could tell by his fast gait and determined look on his face that something was very wrong.

I went outside to meet him.

Sternly he said, "We have to pack up quickly and get out of here!"

"Why? What's going on?" Fear roiled inside me.

He ignored my question, but repeated, "I said we have to pack up quickly and get out of here! Or I will be going to jail!"

My mind reeled. I couldn't even begin to imagine what was happening.

Walter yanked things down or off and threw things into the motorhome without preparing them for storage and travel as he always did. The floor of our motorhome was a jumbled mass of hoses and electrical cords, as well as bicycles and a myriad of other things that we kept outside. Within minutes we were on our way out of town.

"Where are we going?" I quietly asked.

Part of me just wanted to run. If it hadn't been that we had three toddlers aboard, I probably would have. I, who was usually quiet and even-keeled, was in a near panic with fear.

"We are going to 'Elizabeth's' house. We'll talk then."

Elizabeth was the elderly widow lady who owned the motorhome, but let us borrow it for deputation. It was less than an hour's drive away. The drive there was eerily quiet.

When we arrived at Elizabeth's, Walter took our children and went inside. He asked me to stay in the motorhome so we could talk.

Walter told Elizabeth an "emergency" had come up and we would need to park at her home for just a couple of days if she didn't mind. He also asked her if she could watch our children for a few minutes so he and I could talk uninterrupted. She quickly agreed to both requests. She was like a grandmother to our children and was happy to spend time with them.

Walter came back out to the motorhome. I was already sitting at the table. He took the seat opposite me. He acted like he didn't know where to start.

I didn't speak. I wasn't sure I wanted to hear what

he had to say although I had no idea of the subject of the matter.

Finally, he started speaking.

"The meeting I had with your sister and brother-in-law was about Jason."

I nodded. That information I could handle.

"Jason tried to commit suicide because of me."

Now that I could not handle. However, I remained quiet, searching his face.

"When we were at the YMCA last night, I tried to molest Jason. He got mad at me and ran out of the YMCA. I thought he just ran home, but now I realize he ran to the bridge and was ready to jump off, killing himself. Your sister found him just in time."

That is where I stopped breathing. It seemed Walter was speaking a foreign language, because he continued talking but I could not understand a word he said.

When he stopped talking, neither of us said a word for what seemed like eternity. My mind and body tried to process the meaning, but nothing made sense. I was shutting down inside. He tried to take my hand. I yanked it back and told him not to touch me. It was a knee-jerk reaction.

I jumped up. "I have to get out of here!"

I still couldn't breathe, and it seemed the walls of the motorhome were closing in on me quickly. I had to get outside.

Chapter 8

The next few hours and that night is a complete blur in my mind. I honestly do not remember anything until about the next afternoon.

Walter kept following me around trying to talk to me; I shrugged him off. I didn't want him to touch me. I didn't want to look at him. I absolutely abhorred him at that time.

I do remember sitting in Elizabeth's home. The phone rang, and I answered it for Elizabeth as she had gone grocery shopping. It was my mother again. She knew Elizabeth, as well, and had her phone number. She had guessed we might go there.

My mother asked if I was okay. I said I was. She then asked to speak to Walter. I could not hear my mother, but I could tell Walter was being really chewed out by his responses. Finally, I heard him say, "I guess you would call me bisexual. I like having sex with both men and women."

It was like someone punched me in my stomach. First, I had never heard the term "bisexual" before. But his second statement just about took me under. Just how many "both men and women" were we talking about here?

When Walter got off the phone, I asked him, "You say you are bisexual?"

He quietly said, "Yes."

I said, "Just how many people have you had sex with?"

He said, "Oh, well, that is just a figure of speech. I only tried to molest Jason. I didn't actually do it."

I told him, "Have you ever had sex with any other person other than me?"

"No."

"Is there anything else I need to know? I mean, if there is anything connected to this issue that you have been involved with at any time, I need to know it right now . . . because I can't ever go through anything like this again. You need to tell me everything right now!"

"There is nothing more to tell you."

I said, "So, you are saying this was a one-time thing?"

He responded, "Yes, it was a one-time thing. I don't know what came over me. I promise it will never happen again."

I went on to tell him that my trust of him was completely broken and I didn't know if I could ever get it back. He explained he didn't want our marriage to end. I told him I could not go to Australia at that time. There was too much up in the air, and I couldn't leave the country with our children and all. I told him I didn't even know if I could continue in our marriage; I needed time. He said he would give me any time I needed but that I could be assured it was a one-time thing that he couldn't explain how it even happened.

It was more than six months before I could even tolerate his touching my hand. I never fully regained my trust in him.

I asked him if my sister and brother-in-law threatened to call the law. He said they had told him if he left right then and never saw them again, they would not call the law. What would happen to me and the children if he was arrested? We didn't have a house or a vehicle; we basically had no material possessions other than our clothes; I didn't have a job or a way to find one. We had been uprooted for 14 months, so there was no place we actually called home.

Part of me was glad of that for the sake of myself and our children my sister and brother-in-law would not call the law, but part of me wondered at that at the same time: I believed if Walter was not my husband and he had done that to one of my children, I would be the one in jail. He would be six feet under.

Over the next few years, I was to learn that a homosexual or a pedophile who has not been fully found out will buy time by claiming "they didn't actually act on their impulses" and that it was a "one-time thing that I promise will never happen again." It sounds much like an alcoholic who says they are not drinking any more but, in fact, never stopped.

Walter was so well liked among his large network of pastors and other church workers that he soon found a church to pastor. We were headed to Georgia.

I had been very close to my mother prior to this. This incident, however, put a huge rift between us. She couldn't figure out why I didn't immediately leave Walter and divorce him. I told myself that I believed in marriage . . . I didn't want a divorce like my parents had gone through. Before this happened, I loved Walter as much as one human could love another. I had trusted him explicitly. He was the father of my children, and I believed they needed him in their lives in a personal way. I believed his action had literally been a one-time incident that he intended to never let happen again. But if I continued down the road of keeping my marriage with him, I knew it would be at the cost of losing any relationship with my mother, my sister and brother-in-law, and my nephews.

Now, we were living in a strange state, a strange city, starting a new ministry in a strange church where I knew no one; and on top of that, I could not understand a word anyone was saying in their deep Georgian accent! In addition, we did not own a single piece of furniture, dishes, or any household items needed to run a home. I had never felt so alone! There was not a pastor I felt I could talk to, because every one of the ones I personally knew absolutely loved Walter. I did not want to "rat" on him, believing this was a one-time "mistake." I felt like I had to hide Walter's "mistake" to the church we were now working in. I SO BADLY wanted someone to talk to! My soul cried out for a friend. There was no one.

Chapter 9

One day shortly after we arrived in our new hometown, Walter was working at the church. My children were napping. I was standing in the kitchen, mulling over all that had transpired in the last month. Quickly, I became overwhelmed. I had not even had the time to really grieve over the whole mess. I fell hard to my knees in the middle of the kitchen floor. I bent over, placing my head on my hands on the floor and wept like I have never wept in my life. I had thought that losing my daughter had to be the hardest thing I would ever go through. I was wrong.

I wailed and rocked back and forth. I cried out to the Lord to take me. I wanted to die. I started thinking of ways I could take my own life. I didn't want to be in this world any more. It was too ugly; it was too hard. This went on for many minutes. I begged the Lord to let me go Home. I told Him how lonely I was . . . a loneliness that was so big, it could not be contained. I told Him I needed someone to talk to, but there was no one. I pounded the floor with my fist.

Suddenly, one of my children awakened from their nap. I heard them whimper a little at trying to get fully awake. I realized there were three reasons in the next room for me to stay alive. I didn't want Walter to raise them himself. I must be there for them.

I raised up on my knees. I started wiping my face with my hands. Then, in a still, small voice, I heard, "You say you need someone to talk to. I've never left. I'm here. You can talk to me. I am all you need. Family and friends are luxuries; but I am ALL.you.need." For the next several months I started experiencing that fact over and over and over.

The church Walter had started pastoring also had a Christian school. We had approximately 30-35 students from K5 – 12th grade. By the following school year, I was teaching the entire school with a fulltime assistant. Little by little things started getting a little easier in our marriage, although I never ever regained full trust in Walter as I had had before the incident. Time passed; things improved.

Just like in Illinois and in Indiana, Georgia pastors and other church leaders soon became acquainted with Walter and held high regard for him. He was frequently asked to speak at special meetings or conferences. They all loved him.

The teens, especially the boys, in our church were soon tugging and wrestling with Walter just as teens had done in other churches. They idolized him. The parents adored him, not only as their pastor, but as a mentor to their teen boys.

Our church did not have a fulltime secretary, so a church phone was placed in the school classroom, enabling me to handle the rare, incoming call. We went through a period of time of several weeks when the phone would ring and I would answer. The caller would then suddenly hang up. I just chalked it up to a prankster making prank calls.

There was a husband and wife in our church who had four boys, all in our school. The two older boys were in their teens. Walter had spent time with the boys, especially the two teens, and had even gone to their home out in the country when neither of the parents were home because the boys had called him at the church and "needed his help," although the help supposedly needed never made sense to me. The wife, "May," and I became quite good friends. One day she asked me if I would accompany her to another town close by to do a little shopping. I do not like shopping, but I sensed she needed to talk, so I accepted her invitation.

As we pulled into the parking lot and parked the car, she turned off the motor, then simply turned in her seat and looked at me. I didn't know what was on her mind.

She started off, "Have you ever heard of a woman molesting boys?"

She shocked me with the question. I said, "No, I don't believe I have ever heard of that happening, but I guess it could."

She really fidgeted around as she spoke, stumbling to find the words she wanted to say. Finally, she said,

"Well, I just found out my older boys' aunt molested them a while back."

I said, "What?"

She said, "Yes, they finally came to me and told me. They said she lured them into her bedroom where she would molest them. Apparently, she did it several times over a period of time."

I said, "May, I don't know what to say. That is terrible! Have you done anything about it?"

She said, "No, I'm not sure what I should do. That's why I really asked you to come with me shopping. I don't have any shopping to do; I just wanted to get you away from the church and talk to you, so I came up with this excuse."

Then she asked, "Do you know much about people molesting children?"

I really felt uncomfortable at this point, remembering Walter's incident. But then, I rationalized, he told me he only tried to do it and it was a one-time thing. The only thing I personally knew about molestation was what I knew about this lady's pastor. I couldn't tell her that! So, I simply told her I knew next to nothing about the subject. But the discussion certainly left me feeling unsettled. Was May's story really about Walter? I had no proof that Walter had done anything to the boys, but there was just something there that niggled in my brain.

Chapter 10

The "hang-up" phone calls started up again in the school. After a week or two, just as before, they stopped.

Many times, one of the men of the church came to our house and asked to see the pastor. I would explain he was not home, but he had said he would be at the church studying. The one looking for Walter would say, "No, I first called the church and there was no answer. But then I stopped by, and no one was there. It was all locked up." This happened over and over to the point I started wondering what was going on.

Finally, I approached Walter on the subject. I asked him why quite often he wasn't where he said he would be. I explained it was embarrassing for me to tell a deacon or other church member that he was at the church or at another location where he had told me he would be, only to find out he was not there. It was happening often enough that I was getting uncomfortable about people coming and asking where he was. It reminded me of the times church members from our Indiana church would come to our door looking for Walter, and he was nowhere to be found.

When I quizzed Walter about his absences, he brushed me off saying, "Oh, well, it's been so nice outside that I was going to go to the church to study for next Sunday's sermon, but then at the last minute I went to the park so I could study outside."

I asked, "Well, what if there had been an emergency? What if I or the kids needed you? Or what if a church member was in an accident and rushed to the hospital, but we couldn't find you?"

He said, "I'm sorry. I will try from now on to always let you know where I am."

I finally pushed the issue. I told him that ever since the incident with Jason that I had lost trust in him. To rebuild trust, I explained I must be able to ask him anything at any time and get a straight answer from him without his expressing anger toward me over my asking.

"If you get angry, that makes me suspicious. I have to know I can come to you about anything. I need to know where you are at all times."

He told me I could do that, but I could tell he didn't like what I was requesting.

However, over the next months, nothing changed. He still disappeared for hours at a time, and I would not know where he was. If I questioned him about it, he became angry. If someone from the church came looking for him, I started telling the truth: I had no idea where he was or when he was returning.

My suspicions grew, but I had no hard evidence of anything.

One day Walter received a letter in the mail. He seemed excited to hear from someone. He finally brought me a photo of a black man. He told me the letter was from the man, that the man was a childhood friend of his. He said the two of them had run around together during their childhood and teen years. Even though Walter had supposedly not heard from him since their teen years, the man had written to invite Walter to accompany him to the Bahamas for a week. Walter wanted to go. However, he could tell I was not in agreement with his going on the trip—I didn't trust him. He ended up not going, but his wanting to go with someone he had lost touch with for many years added to the suspicions I was accumulating.

We had a troubled teen boy in our school, "Tom." He was in the 10th grade. Tom was known to have a violent side to him. One time, I had given him a detention slip for his behavior. He crumpled it up and threw it in my face. I told him to pick it up. He refused. I told him a second time to pick it up. Instead, he picked up his chair and threw it at me. His father was an ex-Marine and had the air and demeanor of a Marine. He gave the impression you didn't want to mess with him.

Again, it seemed Walter lavished quite a bit of attention on Tom and even gave excuses for him when he misbehaved. I noticed it, but it was always within the classroom, so I didn't think a lot about it.

Walter told me that Tom had asked him one day that if Walter were to die, did he think I would date him. I was deeply puzzled.

I asked Walter, "What caused him to ask such a question?"

Walter just shrugged and said, "I have no idea."

It was just another "incident" that rattled around in my brain as it felt like I was always trying to put a puzzle together without being able to tell what each piece really was. Was Tom's question a veiled threat of some kind to our family?

Chapter 11

We had another teen boy in our school, "Brandon," who really struggled with his school work. His mother was a single parent. I had been working hard with Brandon one-on-one, especially in math. Again, Walter had gone out to Brandon's home to "counsel" him and his mother on several occasions.

I could tell Brandon was really improving in his math. He had a test coming up, and I was hopeful he at least would pass it. Typically, he failed them miserably.

Finally, the test day came. Brandon took the test, but I didn't have time to grade it before the school day ended. Later, that afternoon I ended up in the emergency room, and I was to have emergency gall bladder surgery early the next morning. I took paperwork with me to do in the hospital room. The nurses all made fun of me, grading papers in my bed while I was in so much pain. One of the first papers I pulled out was Brandon's test. I couldn't wait any longer to grade it. He made a 100% on it! I almost screamed in the hospital room; I was so excited for his achievement!

Walter had stepped out to get something to eat. When he returned, I told him the good news.

I suggested, "Please go call Brandon right now. He needs to know! Tell him I am so proud of him!"

Walter seemed not to be that impressed and gave me some excuse that he thought it was too late or something, that he would be sure he was told the following day. I was so disappointed, but I didn't have a way to get a hold of Brandon myself. I had to be patient and wait for the next day.

As soon as I awoke from the anesthesia the following day, I told Walter, "We need to let Brandon know right away about his math test!"

Walter looked grimly at me. He said, "I didn't want to tell you last night. I wanted to wait until after your surgery. But Brandon committed suicide last night."

I never got to tell Brandon he made a 100% on his test. I could not grasp as to why he killed himself when he was improving dramatically in school and everything was looking up for him. Then the picture of my nephew standing on a bridge, ready to commit suicide, came flooding into my mind. Again, I only had suppositions.

One afternoon, Walter told me that Tom's parents had requested he come to their home. They wanted to talk to him about Tom. I just assumed I would go with Walter, since Tom was my student in school. When Walter saw me getting ready to go with him, he stopped me, "Oh, no. They want to see me alone."

I was surprised, but said, "Oh, okay. I'll stay home then."

He left without me and was gone quite a while. When he got back home, he told me, "We need to talk."

The tone in his words cut through me. Sitting at a table in the motorhome some years ago flooded back into my mind.

I sat on the edge of the bed. Walter sat down next to me.

He started, "As you know, I went to see Tom's parents. Tom was there, too. Something happened in the church a few days ago, and Tom went home and told his parents about it. That is what they wanted to talk to me about."

I asked, "What happened?"

Walter said, "Well, Tom and I were alone in the church lobby just talking. Then one thing led to another. We started pushing on one another and finally got in a wrestling match of sorts. While we wrestled around, I reached into his bibbed overalls and his underwear and grabbed his privates."

I closed my eyes. I tried to keep my stomach contents down.

Quickly, Walter added, "I won't ever do it again. I promise!"

I said, "You told me that once before! What is going on? I don't understand all this."

Actually, I could not believe Walter had molested Tom and his ex-Marine father had not killed him! I was amazed he was sitting beside me on the bed all in one piece and not sitting in jail!

I started yelling at Walter. "You told me you would never molest another boy. You told me it was a one-time incident, but clearly it is not! What else have you not told me? The only reason you told me this tonight is because Tom went to his parents! You got caught! How many other times have there been when you were never caught, so you never told me? I feel like I am wasting my life on this marriage."

He swore to me there were no more times, that I knew all there was to know.

I didn't know what to do. All the feelings from the time Walter molested my nephew all came back. I was confused, scared, angry . . . I was shaking! I thought about Brandon.

"Did you ever molest Brandon?"

"No!" he adamantly stated.

Did I believe him? No! But there was no one to back up or to deny his story.

I never knew what transpired or what was said at that meeting at Tom's parents' home. I don't know why Walter, at best, was not arrested or, at worst, killed or beaten.

Tom came to our house a few weeks later, where he molested our son. We did not find out for some time. When our son told us about the incident, he said Tom kept saying, "Your dad did this to me, so I'm doing it to you!" Then it also became clearer as to why Tom had asked Walter that if he died would I date him . . . he was giving a message to Walter that he was planning on hurting our family because Walter had hurt him. Tom ended up going into the military where he later committed suicide.

Chapter 12

A short time after the visit with Tom's parents, Walter told me one evening that he needed to go to Atlanta to visit someone in the hospital there. I asked him who was in the hospital. He answered it was someone I didn't know, that it was a relative of one of our church members who requested he go see them. He said he would be late getting home.

I went to bed at my usual bedtime. I awoke in the middle of the night, and Walter was still not home. I was worried. I couldn't get back to sleep.

Finally, about an hour or so later, I heard him come in the back door. He came straight to our bedroom and flipped on a light.

He said the words I dreaded hearing, "We need to talk."

My heart started pounding. I didn't think I could stand. My mind raced. What could it be now?

We went into the kitchen. He plopped a Polaroid photo down on the counter. It was a photo of me and our children playing in the back yard. We had a fairly large back yard with an above-ground pool and several trees. Beyond the yard was a small creek and then woods. The photo had clearly been taken from the cover of the woods.

I looked at the photo and then at Walter, clearly confused. "What is this?" I asked.

Walter then started telling me a story:

He started by going back to his childhood. He said when he was around nine years of age that a man had lured him into a cornfield in Indianapolis and molested him. From that point on, he started picking Walter up in a van, along with some other young boys, and took them to a motel room where they were put in sexually explicit poses and performed sexual acts while being photographed for pornography purposes. The man, who went by the name of Sam, would then take them back to a location and drop them off so they could go back home. From time to time, Sam would supposedly gather the boys up again and repeat the routine.

Walter explained that Sam always seemed to know where Walter was. He said even when he went to Bible college, Sam contacted Walter, saying it was time for more photographs. They would meet in some nearby motel.

Walter could never figure out how Sam always knew where he was. Walter said Sam had contacted him at every church he worked at, always threatening to let the church or his family know if he didn't cooperate.

Walter asked me, "You know those 'hang-up' calls you got at the school? That was him. He was hoping I would answer the phone. When you answered, he hung up on you. He finally did get a hold of me and told me to meet in a motel in the next town over for photographs. When I met up with him and the photographs taken, he would leave me alone for a while."

He further admitted that the black man in the photo he had shown me earlier was a homosexual man with whom he had had sex multiple times during his teen years.

Walter then picked up the photo of me and our children. He said, "This is a threat. He told me to come to Atlanta for more photographs. I went to meet him tonight. We met in a parking lot where I told him I was not doing it any more. I lied to him and told him that I had already told you about him and the photographs, so he couldn't threaten me with that anymore. I was hoping that would shake him off me. So, he threw down this photograph and said he knew who my wife and children were and where we lived and even had our routine down."

Walter paused. I was sick. I couldn't even stand up. My world spun. I was reeling in fear.

"I need you to know the threat we are faced with. His name, if it is his real name, is Sam. He has thinning red hair and wears gold, wire-framed glasses. He drives a white panel van."

When I could finally speak, I asked him, "What am I supposed to do?"

Walter answered, "Just be careful. Always watch the kids. Keep them close to you; don't let them near the woods. Watch for a white van. If someone comes to the door you don't know, don't answer it!"

I was terrified!

Walter went on to tell me more about his secret, parallel life he had been living since his childhood—way before we had even met. He told me when we lived in Indiana that truckers on I-65 would contact him by radio for him to meet up with them and go into the woods for sex. They actually stashed mattresses in the woods for that purpose. He did this on many occasions he revealed to me. He voluntarily started to tell me in detail what they actually did. He didn't get far when I thought I was going to vomit. I told him I never wanted to hear about any of that ever again! The little he told me before I stopped him played in my mind, wondering if he ever came home to be with me after that. It was too terrible! I found myself literally shaking from shock. I couldn't breathe; I couldn't talk; I couldn't even stand up.

Walter went on to tell me when he went to parks to "study," he was really meeting up with other men.

He told me of "overnight camping" he did in other boys' backyards as kids during which they molested each other. He revealed one night when he was in the eighth grade he and some other boys got angry with one of the boys because he didn't want to "participate" during overnight camping, so he dragged the kid into the woods in Indianapolis and beat him till he thought he was dead. He never knew if he actually killed the kid or not. Was I married to a murderer, as well?

I told Walter I could not understand homosexuality. It was very confusing to me. It seemed he wanted me to understand by saying that no one was born a homosexual; they were recruited into it. It was not about the sex; it was about a mindset, a way of thinking. I could not grasp it. I didn't want to grasp it. I wanted to fling it far from me.

For the next couple of years, I was always hyper-vigilant, scared half to death. I was always looking over my shoulder, keeping my hands on my children or not taking them out at all. If they wanted to play in the back yard, they had to stay up close to the house, and I would be out there with them.

Chapter 13

Soon, Walter decided the "Lord had called him" to move to a different church. I was tired. I was scared. I knew I didn't love Walter any more, of course, but I didn't know what to do. I had no one to turn to. What would be best for my children?

We moved to another town in Georgia where Walter became the pastor of another church. Before long, he resigned at that church and started a brand new church in our home before moving into the building of a former church in that town. He started "disappearing" on me as he had done before.

A new fear popped into my life: AIDS. It was becoming a popular topic with the media. As I heard more and more about it, I became frightened. What about those truckers he met with? What about the men in the parks? Would we both die from AIDS, leaving our children without parents?

That motivated me into knowing the end had come—I had to do something!

I told Walter I was divorcing him. I hired a lawyer

and filed out the paperwork. Walter begged me not to throw away our marriage.

I do not get angry easily. But that day was one day I got so angry, I scared myself. It was a Sunday afternoon. I found our wedding scrapbook full of beautiful photos. I started ripping it into pieces and throwing the pages away from me as I screamed at him. I told him I couldn't believe he so easily threw away what we had, how he destroyed not only our family but so many other families and children. He started to come toward me, telling me not to destroy our photo album. I continued screaming, letting all my pent-up anger loose and telling him he was the one who destroyed the photo album and the memories! I then went and got my wedding dress and shredded it. I threw it out in the garbage in the rain. He kept telling me not to destroy the dress because he knew it had meant so much to me. I screamed back at him, "YOU did it! The dress means nothing anymore!"

Walter went before the church to explain to them I was divorcing him. I didn't hear his speech, but I was told he told the church that several years prior he had committed a "moral sin" that I could never get over or forgive him for. I was divorcing him over it.

Walter was very well loved in the entire town, not just the church. At the time, I didn't know what he told the church. But it wasn't long when I realized each time I would go into the little local grocery store, people would point and whisper. I felt as though I had the letter "A" on the front of my clothes.

Pastors we knew from not only Georgia, but Indiana and Illinois, as well, called me wanting to know why I was divorcing Walter. I simply told them they needed to ask him. A couple of them asked if I wanted to meet with them for "counseling." I felt it would be one-sided: Walter's side! Once again, I really felt alone and abandoned.

I had been a stay-at-home mom, homeschooling our children. Walter took the one vehicle we owned, so I didn't know what I was going to do. I prayed! I then started out on foot to look for a job.

The first place I came to was quite a few blocks from our home, but it was a start. It was a small, weekly newspaper store. I didn't know the owner, but she was pleasant to talk to. I explained to her that I had three children, going through a divorce, and I needed a job immediately. I told her that everywhere I worked, I became a real asset to the company, although I didn't have a resume or references at the moment. She kindly told me her shop was so small that she didn't have any openings. I thanked her for her time and turned to leave. She stopped me and called me back.

She said, "I don't know why I'm doing this. I can't pay you much, but something inside of me is telling me to take a chance on you. Can you come in tomorrow to start?"

My first paycheck was double what she told me she could pay me because she said she would be embarrassed to pay me so little for the work I produced. I worked there several months before moving to Florida. By the time I left, I was doing all their typesetting as well as interviewing and reporting on special feature items, including the Gulf War, for the paper.

While I worked there, I met the sports reporter, "Bill." As a side job, Bill would go to the small-town football, basketball, and baseball games and report on them each week. He would usually come in one night a week and write up his story. Otherwise, he was a well-known, respected realtor in town. He was pleasant enough, but there was not much interaction between him and me. He had actually visited our church one time and remembered me as the piano player there.

One evening before he left the newspaper shop, he stopped at my desk and asked if he could have a moment.

I said, "Sure."

He wanted to know if he could take me to dinner sometime. I believe I was somewhat rude to him as I told him, "No! I'm not even divorced yet!" (I was grasping at straws to turn him down.)

He went on to say he knew my divorce was not final, but that I had filed for it and just waiting for the court date. He wanted to know if I would reconsider and go out to dinner?

I repeated, but a little nicer, "No, thank you."

Unbeknown to me, Bill went to the newspaper owner. They were great friends. He asked her in her opinion how he might get my attention. Together they devised a plan, to which I became privy much later, after the fact.

Here's what they planned: The next day, the newspaper owner said that "of all things," everyone who worked there had a reason they needed to be gone during the same hour that afternoon. She wanted me to be aware I would be there alone and would need to cover the front desk should anyone come in off the street.

I thought it sounded strange, but quickly agreed to her request.

I was busy typesetting, alone in the office, when I heard the front door open. I went around to the front desk to discover Bill standing at the desk.

I was annoyed, but asked him, "May I help you?"

He said, "I would like to take you out for coffee as soon as you finish work today."

I rolled my eyes and said, "No, I don't think so. But thank you."

I turned to leave when he got my attention by what he said next: "Look, I know about you and your husband. I know about your divorce. But what you don't understand is, I know some things you don't know; and your not knowing could bring danger to yourself and to your children. All I am asking is for coffee right across the street right after work."

Something inside me told me I needed to accept, so I did.

As soon as work was over, I went across the street to a little café. I went in and found Bill already sitting at a booth. He got up as I approached. I told him I didn't drink coffee, but I would like a Coke, which he ordered.

Then he told me, "Like I said I have some information you need to know. But let me explain how I got the information first."

I just looked at him, but my heart started pounding. He was scaring me!

He said, "I saw you at your church when I visited, but I didn't come up and introduce myself. Then, later, I heard you and your husband were divorcing. I wanted to know more about you. So I started doing a little research."

I simply kept sitting, listening.

He continued, "My research took an unexpected turn . . . not about you, but about your husband. It took me to Atlanta. He is involved with some pretty heavy stuff that, if you already don't know . . . and I don't think you do . . . you need to know!"

My nerves were shot; this man was terrifying me. I jumped up, not even touching my Coke.

I told him, "I already know enough to divorce him! I don't need or want to know anything more. You don't understand . . . I can't take any more!"

I turned and started for the door. He all but yelled to my back, "I'm telling you that you and your children could be in grave danger. You need to hear me out!"

I left the café and never looked back. I was shaking so hard I could barely get myself home.

To this day, I still do not know what it was he was going to tell me. Sometimes, I wish I had been courageous enough to hear him out. But my mind and body were shutting down. I didn't know how much more I could take.

At last, the divorce became final. However, because of his popularity, quite a few church members, as well as other friends and acquaintances, expressed to me their disbelief at my divorcing such a "wonderful man," a "doting husband," and a "great father." They thought I was "lucky" to have such a man.

All I saw was that I was finally free of him . . . or so I thought.

Chapter 14

Several years later, I was living in Florida. A detective contacted my sister who, in turn, contacted me. The detective told my sister he was doing an investigation that involved who they thought was Walter, but they did not have a way to positively identify the man they were following. He wondered if my sister perchance had a photo of him. My sister said she did not have a photo, but maybe I did.

My daughter had a photo of her dad in her room, so I was able to fax it to the detective. I thought that FINALLY justice might be coming to this man who destroyed so many families.

When the detective received the photo, he affirmed Walter was the man they were following. He told me that they considered Walter armed and dangerous. I told him I had no knowledge of Walter ever owning a gun, at least during our marriage . . . but then, there was a lot I didn't know about him during our marriage!

The detective went on to say that "something" was going down that weekend involving Walter and the active investigation, so I was to be sure my children were not anywhere around where Walter was going to be.

I told the detective, "Whoa! Wait up! He is supposed to pick up my children for the weekend! I will have to come up with some excuse that they cannot go this weekend."

The detective sounded alarmed. "No, don't change your plans; we'll change ours. If you change your plans, he may suspect something is up. We'll just make our move another time. Keep everything as you already planned. We'll hold up."

That was the last time I heard from the detective.

Afterword

Today, Walter is "married" to a man and lives in the Orlando area. Why is he not sitting in prison? How is it that he destroyed so many lives and still walks free? I believe he molests still when given the opportunity because that is what a sexual predator does, but I have no proof.

Walter is bisexual by his own admission. He is a pedophile by his own admission. He is a sexual predator by his own admission. Yet he walks free.

My son once asked him, "Why did you marry Mom if you already knew you were bisexual and a child molester?"

His answer was, "Because I wanted children. So I chose her because she was raised in a strict, Christian home with an overbearing mother, and I knew she was naïve enough that I could easily hide my secret life from her." It made me feel like I had only been an object for him, never loved as I thought I had been. My "fairy tale" marriage was a figment of my imagination! I was just another of his victims . . . until I stopped him in my life.

Where are all his other victims? Why have they or their parents not pressed charges? Are they too afraid of him? Why are the statute of limitations in these matters so short, especially since they affect a victim's life for the rest of their life? If someone knows something about a person's being a sexual predator, a pedophile, why can't that person come forward and be taken seriously, even if the crime wasn't against them personally?

I have talked with several law enforcement officers over the years and at least one lawyer. They all have told me I cannot do anything on my own; that no crimes were committed against me personally. I can be a witness; but I cannot be a plaintiff. I've had law enforcement say they will look into it or have said they know someone in the department who has "connections" who would look into it, but nothing has ever come from any of it.

Who is protecting him? Why are they protecting him? Is it part of a human trafficking network?

I have lots of questions. I have not many answers.

What I can say for sure, though, is that I went into this spiritual battle as a fragile, quiet, naïve, shy little girl—the type for whom he was looking . . . but after years of mental and physical warfare, I emerged a warrior!

**If you appreciated this book,
I would be extremely grateful if you would leave
a brief review on Amazon at:**

https://www.amazon.com/Not-My-Shame-True-Story/dp/B0863S4NPT

To connect with Sheila:

**sheilaraeboyd@gmail.com
https://www.facebook.com/sheilaraeboyd/**

Made in the USA
Coppell, TX
24 April 2023